Bird Watching Log Book

Copyright © Hayden Macfarland
All Rights Reserved.
No part of this publication can be used or reproduced in any manner whatsoever without written permission except in the case of brief quotations embodied in critical articles and reviews.
First Edition: 2021

This Journal Belongs to:

_____

Bird Log

Season	Bird Name

Date	Time

Weather Conditions

Place Seen

Bird Behavior

Features/Description

Notes

Bird Log

Season	Bird Name

Date	Time

Weather Condition

Place Seen

Bird Behavior

Features/Description

Notes

Bird Log

Season	Bird Name

Date	Time

Weather Conditions

Place Seen

Bird Behavior

Features/Description

Notes

Bird Log

Season	Bird Name

Date	Time

Weather Condition

Place Seen

Bird Behavior

Features/Description

Notes

Bird Log

Season	Bird Name

Date	Time

Weather Conditions

Place Seen

Bird Behavior

Features/Description

Notes

Bird Log

Season	Bird Name

Date	Time

Weather Condition

Place Seen

Bird Behavior

Features/Description

Notes

Bird Log

Season	Bird Name

Date	Time

Weather Conditions

Place Seen

Bird Behavior

Features/Description

Notes

Bird Log

Season	Bird Name

Date	Time

Weather Condition

Place Seen

Bird Behavior

Features/Description

Notes

Bird Log

| Season | Bird Name |

| Date | Time |

Weather Conditions

Place Seen

Bird Behavior

Features/Description

Notes

Bird Log

Season	Bird Name

Date	Time

Weather Condition

Place Seen

Bird Behavior

Features/Description

Notes

Bird Log

Season	Bird Name

Date	Time

Weather Conditions

Place Seen

Bird Behavior

Features/Description

Notes

Bird Log

Season	Bird Name

Date	Time

Weather Condition

Place Seen

Bird Behavior

Features/Description

Notes

Bird Log

Season	Bird Name

Date	Time

Weather Conditions

Place Seen

Bird Behavior

Features/Description

Notes

Bird Log

Season	Bird Name

Date	Time

Weather Condition

Place Seen

Bird Behavior

Features/Description

Notes

Bird Log

Season	Bird Name

Date	Time

Weather Conditions

Place Seen

Bird Behavior

Features/Description

Notes

Bird Log

Season	Bird Name

Date	Time

Weather Condition

Place Seen

Bird Behavior

Features/Description

Notes

Bird Log

| Season | Bird Name |

| Date | Time |

Weather Conditions

Place Seen

Bird Behavior

Features/Description

Notes

Bird Log

Season	Bird Name

Date	Time

Weather Condition

Place Seen

Bird Behavior

Features/Description

Notes

Bird Log

Season	Bird Name

Date	Time

Weather Conditions

Place Seen

Bird Behavior

Features/Description

Notes

Bird Log

Season	Bird Name

Date	Time

Weather Condition

Place Seen

Bird Behavior

Features/Description

Notes

Bird Log

Season	Bird Name

Date	Time

Weather Conditions

Place Seen

Bird Behavior

Features/Description

Notes

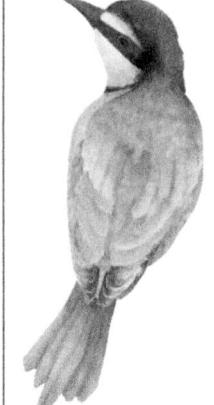

Bird Log

Season	Bird Name

Date	Time

Weather Condition

Place Seen

Bird Behavior

Features/Description

Notes

Bird Log

Season	Bird Name

Date	Time

Weather Conditions

Place Seen

Bird Behavior

Features/Description

Notes

Bird Log

Season	Bird Name

Date	Time

Weather Condition

Place Seen

Bird Behavior

Features/Description

Notes

Bird Log

Season	Bird Name

Date	Time

Weather Conditions

Place Seen

Bird Behavior

Features/Description

Notes

Bird Log

| Season | Bird Name |

| Date | Time |

Weather Condition

Place Seen

Bird Behavior

Features/Description

Notes

Bird Log

Season	Bird Name

Date	Time

Weather Conditions

Place Seen

Bird Behavior

Features/Description

Notes

Bird Log

Season	Bird Name

Date	Time

Weather Condition

Place Seen

Bird Behavior

Features/Description

Notes

Bird Log

Season	Bird Name

Date	Time

Weather Conditions

Place Seen

Bird Behavior

Features/Description

Notes

Bird Log

| Season | Bird Name |

| Date | Time |

Weather Condition

Place Seen

Bird Behavior

Features/Description

Notes

Bird Log

| Season | Bird Name |

| Date | Time |

| Weather Conditions |

| Place Seen |

| Bird Behavior |

| Features/Description |

| Notes |

Bird Log

Season	Bird Name

Date	Time

Weather Condition

Place Seen

Bird Behavior

Features/Description

Notes

Bird Log

Season	Bird Name

Date	Time

Weather Conditions

Place Seen

Bird Behavior

Features/Description

Notes

Bird Log

Season	Bird Name

Date	Time

Weather Condition

Place Seen

Bird Behavior

Features/Description

Notes

Bird Log

| Season | Bird Name |
|---|---|//

Date	Time

Weather Conditions

Place Seen

Bird Behavior

Features/Description

Notes

Bird Log

| Season | Bird Name |

| Date | Time |

| Weather Condition |

| Place Seen |

| Bird Behavior |

| Features/Description |

| Notes |

Bird Log

Season	Bird Name

Date	Time

Weather Conditions

Place Seen

Bird Behavior

Features/Description

Notes

Bird Log

Season	Bird Name

Date	Time

Weather Condition

Place Seen

Bird Behavior

Features/Description

Notes

Bird Log

Season	Bird Name

Date	Time

Weather Conditions

Place Seen

Bird Behavior

Features/Description

Notes

Bird Log

Season	Bird Name

Date	Time

Weather Condition

Place Seen

Bird Behavior

Features/Description

Notes

Bird Log

Season	Bird Name

Date	Time

Weather Conditions

Place Seen

Bird Behavior

Features/Description

Notes

Bird Log

Season	Bird Name

Date	Time

Weather Condition

Place Seen

Bird Behavior

Features/Description

Notes

Bird Log

Season	Bird Name

Date	Time

Weather Conditions

Place Seen

Bird Behavior

Features/Description

Notes

Bird Log

Season	Bird Name

Date	Time

Weather Condition

Place Seen

Bird Behavior

Features/Description

Notes

Bird Log

Season	Bird Name

Date	Time

Weather Conditions

Place Seen

Bird Behavior

Features/Description

Notes

Bird Log

| Season | Bird Name |

| Date | Time |

| Weather Condition |

| Place Seen |

| Bird Behavior |

| Features/Description |

| Notes |

Bird Log

Season	Bird Name

Date	Time

Weather Conditions

Place Seen

Bird Behavior

Features/Description

Notes

Bird Log

Season	Bird Name

Date	Time

Weather Condition

Place Seen

Bird Behavior

Features/Description

Notes

Bird Log

| Season | Bird Name |

| Date | Time |

Weather Conditions

Place Seen

Bird Behavior

Features/Description

Notes

Bird Log

Season	Bird Name

Date	Time

Weather Condition

Place Seen

Bird Behavior

Features/Description

Notes

Bird Log

Season	Bird Name

Date	Time

Weather Conditions

Place Seen

Bird Behavior

Features/Description

Notes

Bird Log

Season	Bird Name

Date	Time

Weather Condition

Place Seen

Bird Behavior

Features/Description

Notes

Bird Log

Season	Bird Name

Date	Time

Weather Conditions

Place Seen

Bird Behavior

Features/Description

Notes

Bird Log

Season	Bird Name

Date	Time

Weather Condition

Place Seen

Bird Behavior

Features/Description

Notes

Bird Log

Season	Bird Name

Date	Time

Weather Conditions

Place Seen

Bird Behavior

Features/Description

Notes

Bird Log

Season	Bird Name

Date	Time

Weather Condition

Place Seen

Bird Behavior

Features/Description

Notes

Bird Log

Season	Bird Name

Date	Time

Weather Conditions

Place Seen

Bird Behavior

Features/Description

Notes

Bird Log

Season	Bird Name

Date	Time

Weather Condition

Place Seen

Bird Behavior

Features/Description

Notes

Bird Log

Season	Bird Name

Date	Time

Weather Conditions

Place Seen

Bird Behavior

Features/Description

Notes

Bird Log

Season	Bird Name

Date	Time

Weather Condition

Place Seen

Bird Behavior

Features/Description

Notes

Bird Log

Season	Bird Name

Date	Time

Weather Conditions

Place Seen

Bird Behavior

Features/Description

Notes

Bird Log

Season	Bird Name

Date	Time

Weather Condition

Place Seen

Bird Behavior

Features/Description

Notes

Bird Log

Season	Bird Name

Date	Time

Weather Conditions

Place Seen

Bird Behavior

Features/Description

Notes

Bird Log

Season	Bird Name

Date	Time

Weather Condition

Place Seen

Bird Behavior

Features/Description

Notes

Bird Log

Season	Bird Name

Date	Time

Weather Conditions

Place Seen

Bird Behavior

Features/Description

Notes

Bird Log

Season	Bird Name

Date	Time

Weather Condition

Place Seen

Bird Behavior

Features/Description

Notes

Bird Log

Season	Bird Name

Date	Time

Weather Conditions

Place Seen

Bird Behavior

Features/Description

Notes

Bird Log

| Season | Bird Name |

| Date | Time |

Weather Condition

Place Seen

Bird Behavior

Features/Description

Notes

Bird Log

Season	Bird Name

Date	Time

Weather Conditions

Place Seen

Bird Behavior

Features/Description

Notes

Bird Log

| Season | Bird Name |

| Date | Time |

Weather Condition

Place Seen

Bird Behavior

Features/Description

Notes

Bird Log

Season	Bird Name

Date	Time

Weather Conditions

Place Seen

Bird Behavior

Features/Description

Notes

Bird Log

| Season | Bird Name |

| Date | Time |

| Weather Condition |

| Place Seen |

| Bird Behavior |

| Features/Description |

| Notes |

Bird Log

| Season | Bird Name |

| Date | Time |

| Weather Conditions |

| Place Seen |

| Bird Behavior |

| Features/Description |

| Notes |

Bird Log

Season	Bird Name

Date	Time

Weather Condition

Place Seen

Bird Behavior

Features/Description

Notes

Bird Log

Season	Bird Name

Date	Time

Weather Conditions

Place Seen

Bird Behavior

Features/Description

Notes

Bird Log

Season	Bird Name

Date	Time

Weather Condition

Place Seen

Bird Behavior

Features/Description

Notes

Bird Log

Season	Bird Name

Date	Time

Weather Conditions

Place Seen

Bird Behavior

Features/Description

Notes

Bird Log

Season	Bird Name

Date	Time

Weather Condition

Place Seen

Bird Behavior

Features/Description

Notes

Bird Log

Season	Bird Name

Date	Time

Weather Conditions

Place Seen

Bird Behavior

Features/Description

Notes

Bird Log

Season	Bird Name

Date	Time

Weather Condition

Place Seen

Bird Behavior

Features/Description

Notes

Bird Log

Season	Bird Name

Date	Time

Weather Conditions

Place Seen

Bird Behavior

Features/Description

Notes

Bird Log

Season	Bird Name

Date	Time

Weather Condition

Place Seen

Bird Behavior

Features/Description

Notes

Bird Log

Season	Bird Name

Date	Time

Weather Conditions

Place Seen

Bird Behavior

Features/Description

Notes

Bird Log

Season	Bird Name

Date	Time

Weather Condition

Place Seen

Bird Behavior

Features/Description

Notes

Bird Log

Season	Bird Name

Date	Time

Weather Conditions

Place Seen

Bird Behavior

Features/Description

Notes

Bird Log

Season	Bird Name

Date	Time

Weather Condition

Place Seen

Bird Behavior

Features/Description

Notes

Bird Log

Season	Bird Name

Date	Time

Weather Conditions

Place Seen

Bird Behavior

Features/Description

Notes

Bird Log

Season	Bird Name

Date	Time

Weather Condition

Place Seen

Bird Behavior

Features/Description

Notes

Bird Log

| Season | Bird Name |

| Date | Time |

Weather Conditions

Place Seen

Bird Behavior

Features/Description

Notes

Bird Log

Season	Bird Name

Date	Time

Weather Condition

Place Seen

Bird Behavior

Features/Description

Notes

Bird Log

Season	Bird Name

Date	Time

Weather Conditions

Place Seen

Bird Behavior

Features/Description

Notes

Bird Log

Season	Bird Name

Date	Time

Weather Condition

Place Seen

Bird Behavior

Features/Description

Notes

Bird Log

Season	Bird Name

Date	Time

Weather Conditions

Place Seen

Bird Behavior

Features/Description

Notes

Bird Log

Season	Bird Name

Date	Time

Weather Condition

Place Seen

Bird Behavior

Features/Description

Notes

Bird Log

Season	Bird Name

Date	Time

Weather Conditions

Place Seen

Bird Behavior

Features/Description

Notes

Bird Log

Season	Bird Name

Date	Time

Weather Condition

Place Seen

Bird Behavior

Features/Description

Notes

Bird Log

Season	Bird Name

Date	Time

Weather Conditions

Place Seen

Bird Behavior

Features/Description

Notes

Bird Log

Season	Bird Name

Date	Time

Weather Condition

Place Seen

Bird Behavior

Features/Description

Notes

Bird Log

Season	Bird Name

Date	Time

Weather Conditions

Place Seen

Bird Behavior

Features/Description

Notes

Bird Log

Season	Bird Name

Date	Time

Weather Condition

Place Seen

Bird Behavior

Features/Description

Notes

Bird Log

| Season | Bird Name |

| Date | Time |

Weather Conditions

Place Seen

Bird Behavior

Features/Description

Notes

Bird Log

| Season | Bird Name |

| Date | Time |

Weather Condition

Place Seen

Bird Behavior

Features/Description

Notes

Bird Log

Season	Bird Name

Date	Time

Weather Conditions

Place Seen

Bird Behavior

Features/Description

Notes

Bird Log

Season	Bird Name

Date	Time

Weather Condition

Place Seen

Bird Behavior

Features/Description

Notes

Bird Log

Season	Bird Name

Date	Time

Weather Conditions

Place Seen

Bird Behavior

Features/Description

Notes

Bird Log

Season	Bird Name

Date	Time

Weather Condition

Place Seen

Bird Behavior

Features/Description

Notes

Bird Log

Season	Bird Name

Date	Time

Weather Conditions

Place Seen

Bird Behavior

Features/Description

Notes

Bird Log

| Season | Bird Name |

| Date | Time |

| Weather Condition |

| Place Seen |

| Bird Behavior |

| Features/Description |

| Notes |

Bird Log

Season	Bird Name

Date	Time

Weather Conditions

Place Seen

Bird Behavior

Features/Description

Notes

Bird Log

Season	Bird Name

Date	Time

Weather Condition

Place Seen

Bird Behavior

Features/Description

Notes

Bird Log

Season	Bird Name

Date	Time

Weather Conditions

Place Seen

Bird Behavior

Features/Description

Notes

Bird Log

Season	Bird Name

Date	Time

Weather Condition

Place Seen

Bird Behavior

Features/Description

Notes

Bird Log

| Season | Bird Name |

| Date | Time |

Weather Conditions

Place Seen

Bird Behavior

Features/Description

Notes

Bird Log

| Season | Bird Name |

| Date | Time |

| Weather Condition |

| Place Seen |

| Bird Behavior |

| Features/Description |

| Notes |

Bird Log

Season	Bird Name

Date	Time

Weather Conditions

Place Seen

Bird Behavior

Features/Description

Notes

Bird Log

Season	Bird Name

Date	Time

Weather Condition

Place Seen

Bird Behavior

Features/Description

Notes

Bird Log

Season	Bird Name

Date	Time

Weather Conditions

Place Seen

Bird Behavior

Features/Description

Notes

Bird Log

| Season | Bird Name |

| Date | Time |

Weather Condition

Place Seen

Bird Behavior

Features/Description

Notes

Bird Log

Season	Bird Name

Date	Time

Weather Conditions

Place Seen

Bird Behavior

Features/Description

Notes

Bird Log

Season	Bird Name

Date	Time

Weather Condition

Place Seen

Bird Behavior

Features/Description

Notes

Bird Log

Season	Bird Name

Date	Time

Weather Conditions

Place Seen

Bird Behavior

Features/Description

Notes

Bird Log

Season	Bird Name

Date	Time

Weather Condition

Place Seen

Bird Behavior

Features/Description

Notes

Bird Log

Season	Bird Name

Date	Time

Weather Conditions

Place Seen

Bird Behavior

Features/Description

Notes

Bird Log

Season	Bird Name

Date	Time

Weather Condition

Place Seen

Bird Behavior

Features/Description

Notes

Printed in Great Britain
by Amazon